Gardening Guides

Edible Gardening

GROWING YOUR OWN VEGETABLES, FRUITS, AND MORE

by Lisa J. Amstutz

CAPSTONE PRESS
a capstone imprint

Snap Books are published by Capstone Press,
1710 Roe Crest Drive, North Mankato, Minnesota 56003
www.mycapstone.com

Library of Congress Cataloging-in-Publication Data
Amstutz, Lisa J., author.
  Edible gardening : growing your own vegetables, fruits, and more / Lisa J.
Amstutz.
      pages cm. — (Gardening guides)
  Audience: Ages 8–14.
  Audience: Grades 4 to 6.
  Summary: "Provides readers with gardening projects for edible plants"—
Provided by publisher.
  Includes bibliographical references.
  ISBN 978-1-4914-8235-3 (library binding)
  ISBN 978-1-4914-8625-2 (eBook PDF)
  1. Vegetable gardening—Juvenile literature. 2. Gardening—Juvenile
literature. 3. Plants, Edible—Juvenile literature. I. Title.
  SB324.A47 2016
  635—dc23

Editorial Credits
Abby Colich, editor; Bobbie Nuytten and Tracy McCabe, designers;
Morgan Walters and Tracy Cummins, media researchers;
Laura Manthe, production specialist

Image Credits
All photographs by Capstone Studio: Karon Dubke with the exception of:
Shutterstock: Africa Studio, 12 Middle, Aivolie, 15 Top Middle, Andrey_
Kuzmin (soil), Antonova Anna, Back Cover, Bildagentur Zoonar GmbH, 12
Front, cynoclub, 18 Top Right, Evgeny Karandaev, 7, 10, 27, Kirill Demchenko,
15 Bottom, Luminis, 18 Top Left, Madlen, Back Cover, manulito, 12 Back,
MR.MITR SRILACHAI, 11, Smit, 13, Snowbelle, 15 Bottom Middle, spaxiax,
18 Bottom Right, Studio Barcelona, Back Cover, 19, 20, TRL, 15 Top, verca, 5,
Volosina, 25 Bottom, 25 Top

Design Elements by Shutterstock

Printed in Canada.
102015   009223FRS16

Table of Contents

Get Growing!

Crunchy carrots. Tart tomatoes. Sweet, sun-ripened strawberries. Is your mouth watering yet? These are just a few of the edible plants you can grow in your backyard or on a patio or windowsill. You'll be amazed at how tasty homegrown produce can be.

Gardening Basics

You'll need seeds, seedlings, or plants to begin your edible garden. These are available at garden centers, grocery or hardware stores, catalogs, and online. A seedling is a very young plant. If you start with a seedling or plant, you'll need to transfer it from its original container into your garden or pot. If you're growing indoors or in pots outside, organic potting soil will provide plants with the nutrients they need. Choose a spot for your garden or indoor plants with plenty of sunlight throughout the day.

Watering

Plants need plenty of water, but not too much. Water your garden with a watering can, hose, or spray bottle when it's dry. Follow these tips to make sure your garden is getting the right amount of moisture.

- Always water plants right after planting.
- Water the newly planted seeds or seedlings daily for the first week or two.
- Set out a rain gauge or clear container, and measure the amount of water that it collects. If it doesn't rain at least 1 inch (2.5 centimeters) per week, give your garden a good soaking. Outdoor plants may need extra water on very hot days.
- Water outdoor plants in the morning or evening. This keeps the water from evaporating too fast.
- Water indoor plants if the soil feels dry when you poke your finger below the surface.
- Don't overwater your plants. An overwatered plant will look droopy. It could die.

Weeding

Gardens are not difficult to grow, but they do need some care. Here are a few tips on weeding to keep your plants in good shape.

- It can be difficult to tell seedlings from weeds. Plant labels will help you know where you planted each seed. Planting in rows or neat patterns makes it easier to spot the seedlings as well.
- Remove weeds when they are tiny and when the soil is damp. This makes them easier to pull out and disturbs the soil less.
- Pull weeds out by hand, or with a hand cultivator or hoe.
- Remove the roots so the weeds do not grow back.
- Do not leave pulled weeds in the garden. They may put down new roots and regrow.

Mulching

The best way to prevent weeds is to put mulch around your plants. Newspaper, cardboard, wood chips, and straw all make good mulches. They shade the soil so weeds cannot grow. They also keep the soil moist.

Tools

Some gardening projects require a few tools. You can purchase these at a garden center, department store, or hardware store if you don't already own them.

These tools will help you prepare and maintain an outdoor garden bed:

- spade—a long-handled tool used to dig holes for planting and to turn over soil to prepare a bed
- rake—a toothed tool used for smoothing soil and removing rocks and clumps of debris
- hoe—a tool with a flat blade for removing weeds or loosening soil, compost, or manure
- peat moss—organic material that will help plants grow when added to soil

These tools come in handy in many gardens:

- trowel—a hand tool used to dig holes for bulbs or seedlings
- stake—stick or pole used to prop up plants and mark the ends of rows in your garden
- twine—strong string tied to stakes to mark a row or an area you plan to dig up
- plant labels—tags to help you remember what you planted and where
- tomato cage—made of wire, it helps keep tomato and other plants upright

PREPARING AN OUTDOOR GARDEN SITE

Before you can start planting outdoors, you need to prepare the soil. If you're starting a new garden, remove any grass and weeds. Turn and mix the soil well. If you have very sandy or heavy clay soil, mix in some compost, manure, or peat moss. Rake out any clumps of weeds and large stones. Then smooth out the soil. If you've already used the area for a garden, remove any weeds, and then loosen the soil before smoothing it out.

Upside-Down Planter

Amaze your friends by growing plants upside down! You can grow many kinds of veggies in soda bottle planters. Upside-down plants are easy to care for. Most pests can't reach them, and there's little space for weeds to grow.

What You'll Need

- clean 2-liter soda bottle
- utility knife or scissors
- colorful duct tape
- hole punch
- 3 pieces of twine, each about 3 feet (90 cm) long
- pepper plant
- potting soil
- hook or place to hang your plant

Instructions

1. Have an adult help you cut off the bottom of the soda bottle just below the label with a utility knife or scissors. Remove the label by soaking the bottle in hot water.

2. Cover the cut edge of the bottle with duct tape.

3. Punch three holes in the duct tape, spaced evenly around the bottle.

MORE PLANT CHOICES

Many plants grow well in upside-down planters. Try growing herbs, pickling cucumbers, green beans, or cherry tomatoes.

4. String a piece of twine through each hole. Tie the ends of each piece together.

5. Gently slip the pepper plant through the top of the bottle so the plant hangs out and the roots stay inside.

6. Fill the bottle with potting soil, leaving 1 inch (2.5 cm) below the cut end.

7. Hang your planter in a sunny spot on a porch or deck. Water daily through the top opening of the planter. Harvest peppers when they are fully grown.

Microgreen Magic

These baby veggies are packed with nutrients. Microgreens make a great salad topper, sandwich filler, or crunchy snack. They don't need much space, so they're easy to grow indoors.

What You'll Need

- small, shallow container or planter
- potting soil
- 1 packet of organic arugula, basil, broccoli, cabbage, celery, chia, or sunflower seeds (Make sure the seeds are organic. Treated seeds are poisonous.)
- scissors

Instructions

1. Fill container with 2 inches (5 cm) of potting soil.

2. Sprinkle seeds over the soil and press down lightly.

3. Cover seeds with a thin layer of soil, about 1/8 inch (3 millimeters) thick.

4. Place near a sunny window.

5. Using a clean spray bottle, mist the soil with water every day. The seeds should sprout in 3 to 7 days.

6. Harvest your microgreens when they are 1 to 2 inches (2.5 to 5 cm) tall, after the first true leaves have appeared. True leaves appear after the first set of "seed leaves." Snip plants near the roots with scissors.

7. To start a new batch of microgreens, pull out the remaining roots, smooth the soil, and plant more seeds. You can reuse the soil many times.

WHAT ARE SEED LEAVES?

Seed leaves are the first set of leaves to come up through the soil. Some kinds of plants have only one seed leaf. Others have two. Seed leaves feed the baby plant until it can make its own food.

Three Sisters Garden

Beans, squash, and corn are the "three sisters" of a popular American Indian legend. When planted together, each plant helps the other two. The corn supports the beans. The beans take nitrogen from the air and put it into the soil. The squash leaves shade out weeds and keep the soil cool and moist. Their prickly stems help deter pests as well.

What You'll Need

- garden bed, 3 x 3 feet (1 x 1 meter)
- 6 sweet corn seeds
- 6 pole or runner bean seeds
- 1 pumpkin or other squash seed

Instructions

1. Prepare your garden bed in late spring, once the danger of frost has passed.

2. Build a mound of soil on top of the garden bed about 4 inches (10 cm) high.

3. Plant each corn seed about 6 inches (15 cm) from the center of the mound. Space them evenly so they form a circle.

4. When the corn is 4 inches (10 cm) tall, plant each bean seed about 12 inches (30 cm) from the center of the mound. Space them evenly between the corn plants.

5. At the same time, plant the pumpkin or squash seed near the outer edge of the mound.

6. Water garden and remove weeds as needed.

7. As the beans start to grow, be sure the vines climb up the corn. You may need to help them by moving them up around the corn stalk yourself.

8. Harvest corn when the ears feel full and the tassels turn brown. Bean pods should be large and firm. Pumpkins are ripe when the skin is tough and orange.

DID YOU KNOW?

Nitrogen is a chemical that helps plants grow and reproduce. Nitrogen gas makes up 78 percent of Earth's atmosphere.

Time for Tea

Curl up with a good book and a cup of tea! Grow one or more of these refreshing herbal teas. These herbs can be grown indoors or outdoors.

What You'll Need

- 1 deep flowerpot, 8 inches (20 cm) in diameter
- potting soil
- 1 peppermint, spearmint, or lemon balm seedling
- scissors

Instructions

1. Fill pot half-full of potting soil.

2. Remove seedling from its container and set it on top of the soil. Fill in more soil around the plant and press it firmly in place. Leave 1 inch (2.5 cm) of space at the top of the pot.

3. Place your pot in a sunny spot outside or by a sunny window. Water as needed to keep the soil moist.

4. When the plant is bushy and about 6 inches (15 cm) tall, it is ready to harvest. Snip off stems with scissors. Do not remove all the leaves. This will allow the plant to continue to grow.

5. Prepare iced tea with fresh herbs or a cup of hot tea after you've dried the herbs.

For Iced Tea

To prepare iced tea, have an adult help you boil 3/4 cup (150 grams) sugar in 2 cups (470 milliliters) of water. Turn off the burner. Add 1 cup (25 g) of fresh, washed herb leaves. Let them steep for several hours or overnight. Strain out the leaves, and add 6 cups (1.4 liters) of cold water. Chill, add ice, and enjoy.

For Hot Tea

To make hot tea, boil enough water to fill a mug. Using a tea ball, add 1 teaspoon (0.5 g) of dried leaves (see instructions below). Steep for 5 to 10 minutes. If you don't have a tea ball, put the leaves in hot water and strain them out before serving. Add honey or sugar to taste.

DRYING HERBS

To dry herbs for later use, cut off stems near the base. Wrap them together with a rubber band. Hang the bundle upside down on a nail or hook in a cool, dry place. After a week or two, the leaves should be dry and crumbly. Gently pull them off and store them in an airtight container.

Snack Station

Plant a small patch of veggies for snacking. When you get hungry, stop by for a quick munch! If outdoor space is limited, grow your veggies in pots inside.

What You'll Need

- garden bed, 2 x 3 feet (60 x 90 cm)
- trowel
- plant labels
- 12 garden stakes
- 2 tomato cages, 33 inches (84 cm) tall
- 1 packet each of carrot, cucumber, sugar snap pea, lettuce, and radish seeds
- 1 cherry tomato seedling

Instructions

1. Prepare garden bed. Divide into six 1 x 1 foot (30 x 30 cm) squares. Place a stake in the corner of each square to separate.

2. As soon as the soil thaws in spring:

 ✑ Sprinkle lettuce seeds lightly over one square. Cover with a thin layer of soil, about 1/8 inch (3 mm) thick.

 ✑ Plant radish seeds in one square, about 0.5 inch (1.25 cm) deep and 2 inches (5 cm) apart.

 ✑ Set a tomato cage in the center of one square and push it into the ground. Plant sugar snap pea seeds 2 inches (5 cm) apart and 1 inch (2.5 cm) deep in a circle around the cage. The cage will support the plants as they grow.

 ✑ Place plant labels in each square.

3. After danger of frost has passed:

 ✑ Plant tomato seedling. Dig a hole with your trowel in the center of one square, a little deeper than the root ball. Take the seedling out of the container, set it in the hole, and pat soil firmly around it to hold it in place. Set a tomato cage over the plant, and push it into the ground.

 ✑ Sprinkle carrot seeds lightly over one square. Pat down, and cover with a thin layer of soil.

 ✑ Plant three cucumber seeds near the center of the last square, about 1 inch (2.5 cm) apart. Poke each seed about 1 inch (2.5 cm) into the ground, and smooth the soil over it.

 ✑ Place plant labels in each square.

4. Water garden and remove weeds as needed.

5. Once your carrots start growing, thin them out. Pull out smaller seedlings so the ones that are left will be about 3 inches (7.5 cm) apart.

6. Harvest times may vary. Save your seed packets for directions on when to harvest your veggies.

GROWING INDOORS

If you can't grow a snack garden outdoors, plant sugar snap peas, radishes, carrots, lettuce, and cherry tomatoes indoors. Instead of cucumbers, try dwarf French beans. Fill six large pots with potting soil to within 1 inch (2.5 cm) of the top. Follow the instructions for planting as you would for outdoor growing. Set pots near a sunny window or on a patio or balcony.

Spaghetti Garden

You can't actually plant spaghetti noodles, but you can plant the next closest thing—spaghetti squash! Add sauce ingredients, and harvest a *delizioso* Italian dinner! Plant your spaghetti garden in the spring after danger of frost has passed.

What You'll Need

- garden bed, 2 x 3 feet (60 x 90 cm)
- trowel
- 12 garden stakes
- plant labels
- 1 tomato cage, 33 inches (84 cm) tall
- 1 seedling each of Roma tomato, green pepper, basil, and oregano
- 6 onion sets (small bulbs for planting)
- 3 spaghetti squash seeds
- scissors

Instructions

1. Prepare garden bed. Divide into six 1 x 1 foot (30 x 30 cm) squares. Place a stake in the corner of each square to separate.

2. Plant one square each of tomato and pepper seedlings. Dig a hole with your trowel in the center of one square, a little deeper than the root ball. Take the seedling out of the container, set it in the hole, and pat soil firmly around it to hold it in place. Set a tomato cage over the tomato plant and push it into the ground.

3. Plant one square each of basil, oregano, onions, and spaghetti squash. Plant seedlings as in step 2. Press onion sets firmly into the ground to bury them. Cover with soil. Poke spaghetti squash seeds about 1 inch (2.5 cm) into the soil near the center of the last square, 1 inch (2.5 cm) apart. Cover with soil.

4. Place plant labels in each square.

5. Water garden and remove weeds as needed.

6. Harvest tomatoes when they are fully red. Spaghetti squash are ready to harvest when they are cream-colored and the skin is tough. Peppers will be about 4 inches (10 cm) long when ripe. Snip oregano and basil stems with scissors once they are at least 4 inches (10 cm) long and leafy.

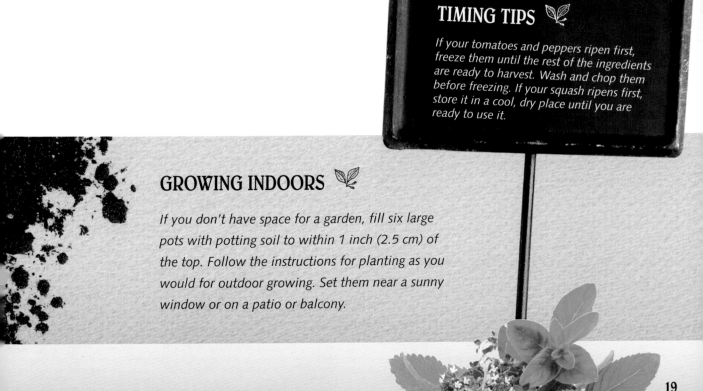

TIMING TIPS

If your tomatoes and peppers ripen first, freeze them until the rest of the ingredients are ready to harvest. Wash and chop them before freezing. If your squash ripens first, store it in a cool, dry place until you are ready to use it.

GROWING INDOORS

If you don't have space for a garden, fill six large pots with potting soil to within 1 inch (2.5 cm) of the top. Follow the instructions for planting as you would for outdoor growing. Set them near a sunny window or on a patio or balcony.

Preparing Your Spaghetti Dinner

Once you've harvested your ingredients, it's time to turn them into dinner. With an adult's help, follow the recipes below to prepare your spaghetti squash and sauce. Add a salad and garlic bread to top off your Italian meal.

Spaghetti Sauce

What You'll Need

- 6 large tomatoes, cut into quarters with stems removed
- 2 green peppers, diced
- 2 large carrots, cut into 1-inch (2.5-cm) pieces
- 1 large onion, cut into quarters
- 1/4 cup (60 mL) olive oil
- 12 cloves fresh garlic
- handful of fresh basil
- handful of fresh oregano
- pinch of salt
- pinch of crushed red pepper (more if desired)
- 9- x 13-inch (23- by 33-cm) baking pan

Instructions

1. Rub pan lightly with olive oil.

2. Chop tomatoes, peppers, carrots, and onion as listed above.

3. Put vegetables, tomatoes, herbs, garlic, salt, and crushed red pepper in baking pan and stir.

4. Roast in oven at 450°F (230°C) for 1 to 1½ hours, until the juices thicken. Stir every 15 minutes. The tomatoes may blacken a bit.

5. Remove pan from oven and let the sauce cool. Run it through a food mill or puree it in a blender if you'd like a smoother texture.

Spaghetti Squash

What You'll Need

- knife
- spoon
- olive oil
- pinch of salt and pepper
- baking dish
- ½ cup (118 mL) water

Instructions

1. Wash the spaghetti squash and have an adult cut it in half lengthwise. Scrape out the seeds with a spoon.

2. Drizzle squash with olive oil and sprinkle with salt and pepper.

3. Set the squash in a baking dish with the cut sides down. Pour water into the dish.

4. Bake at 425°F (220°C) for 45 to 60 minutes.

5. Cooked squash should feel soft when you stick a fork in it. Gently scrape out the "spaghetti" strands with a fork and place on plate. Top your spaghetti squash with sauce and enjoy.

Edible Flower Garden

Did you know there are flowers you can eat? Sprinkle edible flower petals on a salad or cupcake, or freeze them in ice cubes to dress up your lemonade.

What You'll Need

- 4 terra-cotta flowerpots, 6 inches (15 cm) in diameter
- potting soil
- 1 packet each of calendula, pansy, violet, and nasturtium (Copper Sunset or Whirlybird) seeds
- plant labels

Instructions

1. Fill pots with potting soil to 1 inch (2.5 cm) below the rim.
2. Sprinkle flower seeds in each pot and pat them down.
3. Place plant label in each pot.
4. Cover the seeds with a thin layer of soil, about 1/8 inch (3 mm) thick.
5. Place pots on a sunny windowsill, patio, or balcony.
6. Water plants as needed to keep the soil moist.
7. Cut or pinch off the blossoms after they open.

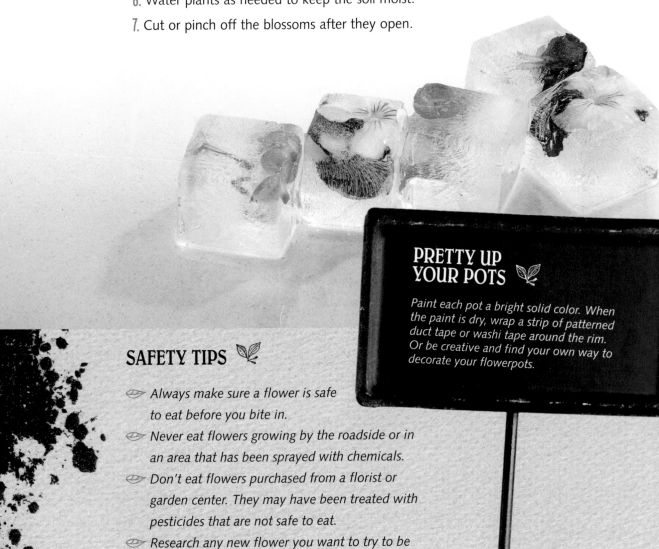

PRETTY UP YOUR POTS

Paint each pot a bright solid color. When the paint is dry, wrap a strip of patterned duct tape or washi tape around the rim. Or be creative and find your own way to decorate your flowerpots.

SAFETY TIPS

- Always make sure a flower is safe to eat before you bite in.
- Never eat flowers growing by the roadside or in an area that has been sprayed with chemicals.
- Don't eat flowers purchased from a florist or garden center. They may have been treated with pesticides that are not safe to eat.
- Research any new flower you want to try to be sure it is safe. Only eat the parts listed as edible. Other parts of the plant may be poisonous.

Lettuce Tower

If you don't have room for your garden on the ground, try growing it in the air. Turn old soda bottles into an amazing vertical garden.

What You'll Need

- 5 clean 2-liter soda bottles
- utility knife or scissors
- potting soil
- 1 packet lettuce seeds or 4 lettuce seedlings
- twine
- nail and hammer
- fence, post, or other place to tie your garden

Instructions

1. Have an adult help you cut off the bottom 1 inch (2.5 cm) of one bottle with knife or scissors.

2. Using scissors, poke 2 drainage holes about 3 inches (7.5 cm) from the cap on opposite sides of the bottle.

3. Make sure the lid is screwed on tightly. Fill with potting soil to 1 inch (2.5 cm) below the cut end.

4. Wrap twine around the bottle, tying it to a post or fence.

5. Cut off the bottom of the second bottle, and fill with soil as in step 3. Remove cap. Place the nozzle into the soil of the first bottle. Attach to the post or fence with twine.

6. Add two more bottles, repeating step 5 for each.

7. Have an adult help you cut the last bottle in half to make a watering funnel. Remove the cap. Poke a hole in the end of the cap with a nail and hammer. Screw the cap back on. Fill the bottle with water.

8. Cut two vertical 1.5-inch (3.8-cm) slits 1.5 inches (3.8 cm) apart near the center of the first four bottles. Cut a horizontal slit to connect the top edges of the slits. The cuts should form a flap. Bend down each flap.

9. Plant four lettuce seeds or one seedling in each opening.

10. Add water to the funnel. Refill when it gets low.

11. Harvest your lettuce before leaves get too large and tough. Have an adult use a clean, sharp knife or scissors to snip it off at the base. Rinse and store lettuce in a plastic bag up to one week in the fridge until you are ready to use it.

MORE PLANT OPTIONS

Try growing other small plants such as radishes, beets, arugula, parsley, basil, or strawberries in bottle towers.

"Berry" Yummy Garden

Berries are packed with nutrients and flavor. Grow your own berries in pots for sweet snacking. Your plants may not produce much the first year. But if you take good care of them, they will give you berries for years to come!

What You'll Need

- 4 large pots, 12 to 18 inches (30 to 46 cm) in diameter
- potting soil
- trowel
- 9 bamboo garden stakes, 30 inches (76 cm) tall
- twine
- 1 raspberry, 1 thornless blackberry, and 1 gooseberry plant
- 4 strawberry plants

Instructions

1. Fill pots with potting soil to 1 inch (2.5 cm) below the rim.

2. Use a trowel to dig a hole a few inches deeper than the roots. Remove raspberry plant from container and set plant inside the hole.

3. Fill in the hole and press the soil firmly to hold the plant in place. Push three bamboo stakes into the soil around it.

4. Repeat steps 2 and 3 for blackberry and gooseberry plants.

5. As the plants grow, tie them loosely to the stakes with twine. This will keep them from falling over.

6. For strawberry plants, push your trowel into the soil and rock it back and forth to create a narrow opening.

7. Remove one strawberry plant from container and slip the roots into the soil. Press the soil around the plant firmly to hold it in place.

8. Repeat steps 6 and 7 for the remaining 3 strawberry plants.

9. Set pots in a sunny spot. Water and remove weeds as needed.

10. Harvest when the fruit is ripe.

GROWING INDOORS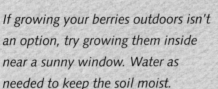

If growing your berries outdoors isn't an option, try growing them inside near a sunny window. Water as needed to keep the soil moist.

Winter Garden

Most cold-climate gardeners hang up their rakes sometime around October. But autumn doesn't have to be the end! Enjoy fresh greens until December or beyond with a simple straw cold frame. Plant your winter garden in early fall.

What You'll Need

- garden bed, 16 x 32 inches (40 x 80 cm)
- 6 rectangular bales of straw (If you don't have access to straw, use 8 double-celled cinder blocks.)
- mulch or soil (optional)
- 1 packet each of spinach, lettuce, mâche, and kale seeds
- clear, heavy plastic sheeting or old storm windows, large enough to cover the area enclosed by the straw
- heavy rocks or bricks

Instructions

1. Prepare garden bed.

2. Sprinkle seeds over the soil. Pat down lightly and cover with a thin layer of soil, about 1/8 inch (3 mm) thick.

3. Set straw or cinder blocks in a rectangle around the bed. If using cinder blocks, place them with the holes facing up. Fill in the holes with mulch or soil to add insulation.

4. Water your seeds well.

5. Cover the garden bed with the plastic or old windows. If you use plastic, weigh down the edges with heavy rocks or bricks.

6. If you live in a hot, dry climate, water your plants when the soil feels dry. In damp climates, enough moisture should collect inside the cold frame. Remove weeds regularly. On warm days, prop up the cover with a stick or remove it so the plants don't overheat.

7. Harvest lettuce and spinach when they are 4 to 6 inches (10 to 15 cm) tall. Mâche grows to only about 2 inches (5 cm) in height. Kale may grow up to 10 inches (25 cm) tall, depending on the variety. Plants may be harvested until late fall or early winter.

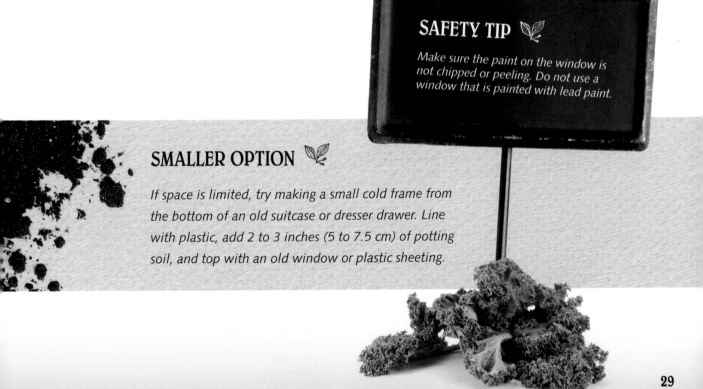

SAFETY TIP

Make sure the paint on the window is not chipped or peeling. Do not use a window that is painted with lead paint.

SMALLER OPTION

If space is limited, try making a small cold frame from the bottom of an old suitcase or dresser drawer. Line with plastic, add 2 to 3 inches (5 to 7.5 cm) of potting soil, and top with an old window or plastic sheeting.

Scrappy Kitchen Garden

Start a garden from your leftover kitchen scraps. It's fun—and free!
Regrow celery and green onion ends and eat them again.

What You'll Need

- 2 shallow dishes
- 1 medium pot about 6 inches (15 cm) in diameter
- potting soil
- root ends of celery and green onion
- water

Instructions for Celery

1. Save about 2 inches (5 cm) of the base of a bunch of celery. Set it in a shallow dish of water. Change water daily to keep it fresh.

2. After a week, transfer the celery to a pot or garden. Cover all but the tips with soil.

3. Water your celery plant as needed.

4. Harvest celery when it is about 1 foot (30.5 cm) long.

Instructions for Green Onions

1. Save the root ends from a bunch of green onions.

2. Set roots in a glass of water. Place them in a sunny window. Change the water daily to keep it fresh.

3. Within a few days, the onions should begin to grow back.

4. When onions have grown back, you can eat them and start all over again!

MORE PLANT OPTIONS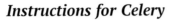

Try regrowing other plants such as lettuce, cabbage, fennel, and leeks this way.

Read More

Brown, Renata Fossen. *Gardening Lab for Kids.* Hands-On Kids. Beverly, Mass.: Quarry Books, 2014.

Hengel, Katherine. *Garden to Table: A Kid's Guide to Planting, Growing, and Preparing Food.* Minneapolis, Minn.: Scarletta Junior Readers, 2014.

Lay, Richard. *A Green Kid's Guide to Soil Preparation.* A Green Kid's Guide to Gardening! Minneapolis, Minn.: Magic Wagon, 2013.

Internet Sites

FactHound offers a safe, fun way to find Internet sites related to this book. All of the sites on FactHound have been researched by our staff.

Here's all you do:

Visit *www.facthound.com*

Type in this code: 9781491482353

Super-cool stuff! Check out projects, games and lots more at
www.capstonekids.com

Books in this series: